I0141784

Hurricane Katrina:

You Can Survive A Natural Disaster!
10 Strategies to Overcome Adversity

Dr. Aaron Joseph Moore Stovall

Dr. Aaron Joseph Moore Stovall

Published by Purpose Publishing
1503 Main Street #168 ✱ Grandview, Missouri
www.purposepublishing.com

ISBN: 978-0-9903010-3-5

Cover design by: Purpose Publishing
Printed in the United States of America

This book is available at quantity discounts for bulk purchases. Inquiries may be addressed to:

PURPOSE PUBLISHING
866-599-6270

*Scripture used in this book are noted
from the KJV of the Bible*

DEDICATION

I would like to dedicate this book to God for saving my life; to my loving brother, Artis, for always providing support and encouragement; to Professor Joyce Williams for sharing her extraordinary creative writing skills in the publication of *College Retreat With Hurricane Katrina*; and to all college students who might experience a hurricane.

Dr. Aaron Joseph Moore Stovall

CONTENTS

Dr. Aaron Joseph Moore Stovall

ACKNOWLEDGMENTS

Special thanks to Mr. Alton Payne and Mr. Floyd Hawkins for the great brainstorming sessions and positive mental attitude. You are cornerstones of creativity at God's Distribution Enterprises, LLC.

Special thanks to Mr. Wayne Hubbard (Host and Producer) and Ms. Candice Price (Founder and CEO) Urban American Outdoor for being leaders in the community. Your sponsorship of the Conservation Summit and other youth activities are phenomenal!

Special thanks to Ms. Cynthia Turner and Dr. Bessie Hampton for editorial assistance.

Special thanks to my mother, Dr. Joyce Moore for prayers, encouragement and editorial assistance.

INTRODUCTION

Aaron Joseph Moore Stovall heard on television about natural disasters killing people in this nation and other countries. At the age of eighteen, Aaron had begun his freshman year at Xavier University of Louisiana. He attended a few days of classes when the strong, most destructive natural disaster in American history, Hurricane Katrina hit New Orleans. The world watched in silence, stunned, as New Orleans was destroyed by the effects of this horrific catastrophe. Now, Aaron was experiencing firsthand the worst hurricane in the history of this country...his life literally flashed before him. This unbelievable experience gave him a different outlook on life.

Aaron Joseph Moore Stovall's book, *College Retreat with Hurricane Katrina* is a personal journal of his six days trapped in a dorm, and how the power of prayer and faith in Jesus Christ enabled him to survive. This intriguing, compelling, thought-provoking journal is a must read. He hopes it will bring inspiration to everyone. It affirms that prayer and faith in Jesus Christ will bring you through any catastrophe. Nothing is too hard or impossible with God.

In Aaron's book, *You Can Survive A Natural Disaster!* he lists 10 strategies that every student attending colleges in regions where hurricanes most frequently occur should read.

STRATEGY 1

Pray and thank God for Safety IN ADVANCE

Thank God in advance for answering your prayers, and for bringing you through adversity safely and swiftly. Our prayers are activated once we KNOW by FAITH they are already answered.

A few weeks prior to attending college, I participated in a weekend retreat at our church entitled, "An Encounter with God." Although hurricane Katrina catapulted me into an overwhelming event, my church retreat prepared me spiritually to go through this natural disaster.

In my Book, *College Retreat with Hurricane Katrina*, on the sixth day, I was safely evacuated with other students by men in a boat and transported to a highway overpass.

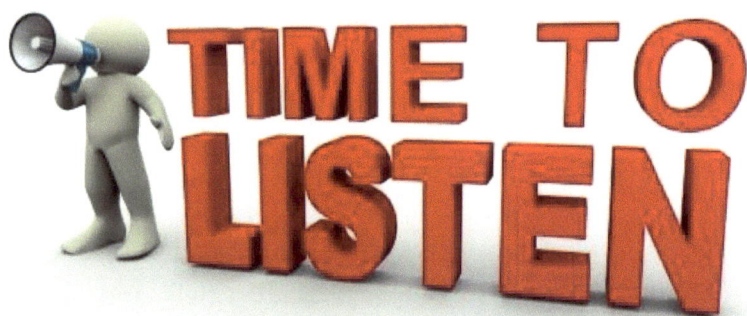

STRATEGY 2

Listen to those in Authority

Always remain coachable in all circumstances. God gave us two ears and one mouth, and we must use them proportionately. God will ensure everything will work out in your favor.

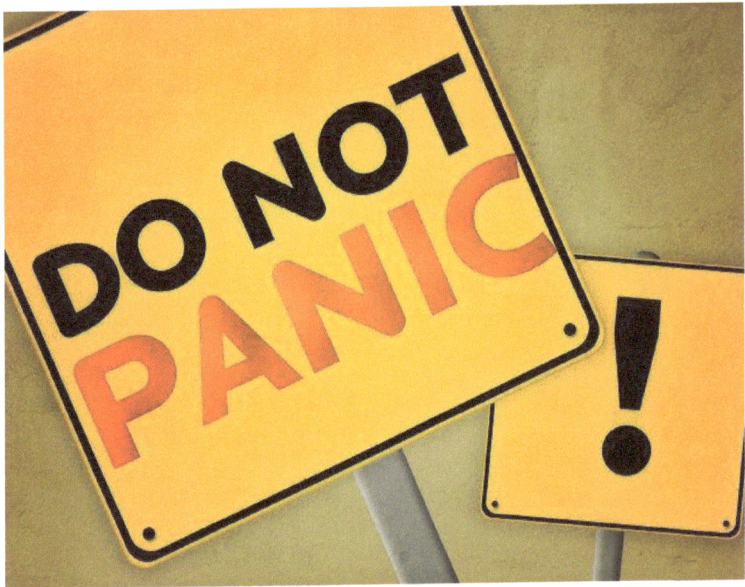

STRATEGY 3

Stay Calm

When you are calm, your mind will allow you to respond rather than react to the situation. Stay calm and know God is with you. Ask God to speak to your heart so that your thoughts and emotions will produce positive feelings.

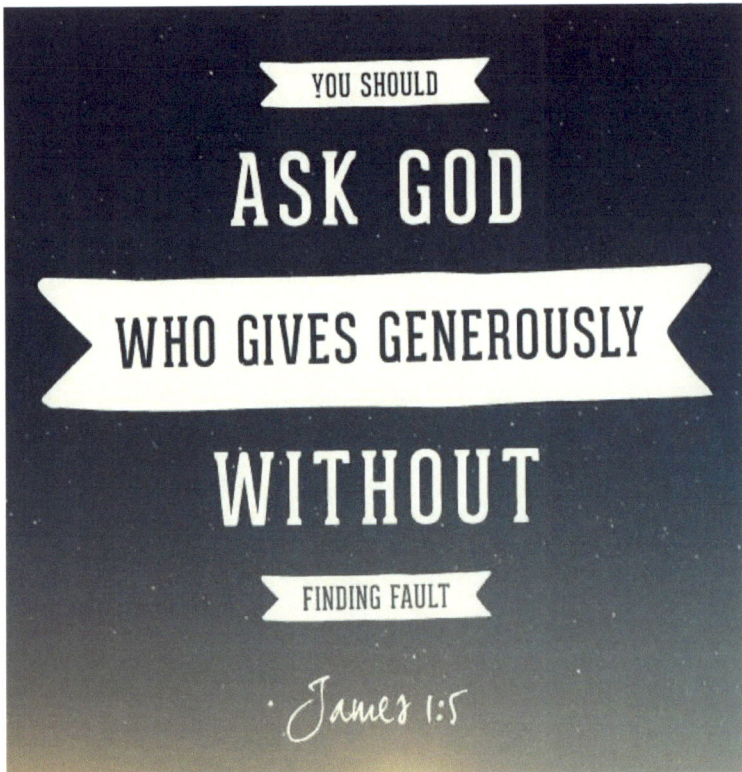

STRATEGY 4

Ask God for Wisdom

Wisdom is the ability to know that things which may appear adverse in the beginning are just seeds for bigger and better opportunities in the end. We must remember, any adverse circumstances we may encounter in our lives, are just preparation for the exciting journey ahead.

It's Time to Call Home!

STRATEGY 5

Immediately Notify Your Family of Your Current Condition

Alert your family and provide them as much pertinent information regarding where you are and your physical condition.

It was my family, friends and church members that prayed for me throughout my retreat with Hurricane Katrina. My Uncle Pete and Aunt Cynthia in Maryland contacted the Mayor of Baltimore as soon as they heard what was going on, and this helped expedite the rescue of the students and me out of Hurricane Katrina.

STRATEGY 6

Positive Mental Attitude

Now faith is the substance of things hoped for, the evidence of things not seen. Hebrews 11:1 KJV

I believe a positive mental attitude is the key to overcoming any and all circumstances life presents. A positive mental attitude allows you to find the gold in any situation. Everyone on this planet is truly blessed, and sometimes we have to remind ourselves of it. Having an "attitude of gratitude" will ensure the best possible outcome no matter your circumstance.

There were times during the storm when I was hungry, fatigued, and frustrated, but I always remained thankful to be alive and well.

SELF CONTROL

STRATEGY 7

Self-Discipline

Remain calculated in all of your actions, which inevitably means act in a way which promotes positivity, peace, and good health to yourself and others.

Acquiring medical attention can be next to impossible in circumstances such as this, and safety should be high on your priority list.

In my Book, *College Retreat with Hurricane Katrina,* on the third night a group of guys watched as one guy lit my hand on fire. In that moment, I completely forgot where I was. I could not believe I had allowed this to happen to me.

Quiet Your Mind!

STRATEGY 8

Meditation

Meditation is a practice most Americans only reserve in times of crisis. The ability to quiet your mind and become present with the "Now" moment is a blessing beyond words. The ability to balance the left and right hemispheres of the brain is really what allows the mind and body to work on one accord. The moment you have control over your thoughts, you will have control over your emotions, and you will inevitably have control of your world. Let's just say the storm is a cake walk at this point.

Intellectual Stimulation

STRATEGY 9

Intellectual Stimulation

There will be a lot of free time to yourself in situations like this. The best thing to do to remain intellectually stimulated is to read, write, or work on puzzles. The more time you spend stimulating your mind intellectually, the less time you have to think about the situation at hand. In addition, you might actually learn or accomplish something new, for example, write a book.

Drink Bottled Water!

STRATEGY 10

Drink Bottled Water

Last but not least, drink bottled water only and eat canned foods. When there is an electrical outage, even for a few hours in warm weather, dairy products, meats, fish and poultry quickly spoil.

Trust in God, and everything will work out in your favor!

REFERENCES

1. Moore Stovall, Aaron Joseph, N.D. *College Retreat with Hurricane Katrina.* AuthorHouse Publishing, Bloomington, Indiana, 2006.

2. *Scripture References:* All scriptures are recommended reading from the King James Version of the Holy Bible.

ABOUT THE AUTHOR

Aaron Joseph Moore Stovall, N.D.

I owe my life to the Lord!!!

Dr. Aaron Joseph Moore Stovall was born in Kansas City, Kansas. He attended elementary, middle and high school in Leavenworth, Kansas. As a student, he excelled academically and became a leader in his community through various extracurricular activities and service projects. He participated in his high school's Peer

Mediation Team where he gave motivational, uplifting lectures to middle school students.

He attended Xavier University on a merit-based scholarship until hurricane Katrina disaster (2005) forced him to transfer to Morehouse College in Atlanta, Georgia. In 2009, Aaron graduated from Morehouse College with his Bachelor of Science degree.

In 2013, he graduated from Southwest College of Naturopathic Medicine and Health Sciences with the degree of Doctor of Naturopathic Medicine. He is the author of *College Retreat with Hurricane Katrina.* Dr. Aaron Moore Stovall is an entrepreneur and motivational speaker.

Contact Dr. Aaron Stovall for speaking engagements at stovallaaron@yahoo.com.

www.ingramcontent.com/pod-product-compliance
Lightning Source LLC
Chambersburg PA
CBHW041756050426
42443CB00023B/14